"Geri's accurate transcription of God's messages brings guidance, growth, and peace for anyone on a spiritual quest."

Sharon Bennett, mentor

Table of Contents

Appreciation i
Introduction 1

• • • Messages • • •

God Announcing Himself 4
High-Tech World 9
Being a Bell 11
Eminent Is Bliss 13
Open Our Hearts 15
Two Entities Merging 17
You Are Unique 19
Divine Design 21
Accepting One Another 23
Love Our Neighbor 25
Sadness and Suffering 27
Plethora of Emotions 29
Business Integrity 33
How Do You Have Time for Me? 37
Spirit All Around 39
Life's Purpose 41
Tackling Our Fears 43
Laws of Love 45
Peace Within 47
Self-Love 49
Importance of Thank You 51
Being Appreciative 53

Lola's Dilemma 55
Physic Hook 57
Benefits of Forgiveness 59
Definition of the Soul 61
A Remembering 63
Dysfunctional Families 65
Hard Economic Times 67
World of Schedules 69
All Denominations Removed 71
Significance of Sunday 73
Jesus, God, and Holy Spirit 75
The Devil 77
Tithing 79
How to View Death 81
How to View Senseless Death 83
How Does This All Work 85
The Light 87

Conclusion 89

• • • God P.S. • • •

What Will *Answers from God* Do for People? 91
How Do You Respond to People Who Think You Are Too Human? 93
What Are Your Thoughts on Documenting Meditations 95
Am I Missing Anything You Would Like Us to Know? 97

*Answers from God Dictionary

In Appreciation

To my mother, Mildred D. Johnsen, for always being there for me. You are the basis for the stability in my life.

To my father, Murel H. Johnsen, for being willing to live with Parkinson's for ten years and teach me the hidden gifts.

To my husband, Arlin, for being the love of my life and allowing me to be me.

To Sharon Bennett, my mentor for twenty-five years, whose unorthodox spiritual style mirrored mine, and who was always a step ahead to guide me.

To CC Salzberg, mentor, who helped me believe in myself.

To Mike Murdock, an evangelist on Day Star, who opened my eyes to "get to know God."

And above all, to God, thank you for trusting me to deliver your beautiful messages of love and comfort safely to the world.

Other Encouraging Hearts

Diane Bump, Lola Leen, Tom Laiche, Pat Moore, Joe and Julie Donoghue, Nancy Johnsen, Doris Toppen, Susan Rendahl, Jerry Bongard, Paul Hirz, Mary Jane Eaton, Toastmasters, Kim Miller, Jo Ferullo, Wilma Monson, Toni Banning, Jan King and Micky Troy

Introduction

I would like to take you on a ride that may surprise you, challenge you, or may even offend you. I am going to ask that you break down barriers of skepticism and go on a journey with me beyond understanding. I ask that you open your heart, mind, and soul to the possibility God can teach in many ways. I ask that you expand your mind to a new thought process, and believe that God can connect with you in a style that fits your profile, that is as natural as breathing.

I was an agnostic over half of my life. I was skeptical; if I couldn't see it, it didn't exist. It seemed so simple, so matter of fact. My childhood lacked any kind of religious training. Mom tried to send us to Sunday school, but Dad would forget to pick us up. That didn't last long. I tried to read the Bible, but I didn't get it. That left me searching for answers using willingness and common sense. What I do remember was a cross that hung on the living room wall. It was the size of my palm, glowed in the dark, and read God Is Love.

I am going to ask that you set aside traditional beliefs of God's teachings. I am talking to those who want a closer relationship with God, one where you spend time with Him to get to know Him. I am talking to those who want to be better and do better but don't know how. I am talking about a relationship with God in which He becomes a friend and a mentor, and you feel His arms around you. A relationship in which you will learn to think differently, act differently, and relate to others differently.

When I had everything I ever wanted I began to wonder if something wasn't missing. I asked myself, "Is there more?" A spiritual thirst began to develop, and I asked anyone who would listen, "What does your spirituality mean to you? What does God want from us?" I read volumes of books searching for purpose and meaning. I discovered what held it all together—*peace within*.

My journey with God has led me to be a born again Christian, where I received answers on the outside to a personal relationship with Him, which gave me answers on the inside. The directness was a style that fit my profile, and one that I could trust. I spent quiet time with God to get to know Him and developed trust in Him. From my dedication, He developed trust in me, and in 2007, I began receiving messages of expanded wisdom from God to make everyday decisions.

In 1985, I received a revelation: God wanted me to write a book called *The Golden Vein of Life: The Common Sense Approach to Spirituality, Simplicity Being the Key*. I ignored His request for over twenty years, and when I finally surrendered and wrote the book, no one got it. I was devastated and disappointed. It sat on the shelf for several years, but the feeling never left. It wasn't until God told me, "I will feed you words of clarity and wisdom that people will relate to and respond to" that I finally understood the power of uniting with God and the things that can be accomplished by trusting Him. That is when I began receiving messages from God. It took me several months to realize that it was the same book God had asked me to write in 1985. I then realized I had changed the title of the book and I asked God, "What do you think about that?" He said, "Well, I like Answers from God, but *the important thing is people see our relationship.*"

It has been a long journey taken in baby steps to trust in God. He has had me out on a limb more times than I can count, and each time I only grew stronger and more confident of Him. *Perception is the key.* The idea that my most loving, intelligent relationship is with someone I cannot see astounds me. I asked God, "How does this all work?" His response was, "You do not need to know how it all works. Do you know how a car works? It just does. I could try and explain it, but we would not be further ahead. In fact, confusion would surely take place. Just know it simply does."

God asked me to write this book. I ask that you believe God is speaking through me. This is my gift from God, dictating messages from God. I feel His love, and I want to share it. I feel His peace, and I want to share it. I want you to have the opportunity to have what I have—a personal relationship with God. He only wants those who are willing. I hope you will be open-minded to a new way of teaching through simplicity, common sense, and a new perception. Willingness is all you need. Join me on my extraordinary ride with God, and see for yourself whether the messages are truthful and meaningful for you. They are sent to you with love.

Geri Cruz

The following message is one of the first clear messages I received.

God is announcing Himself!
God is telling us what we can expect from His messages. It reads like a ticker tape. I never received one like it again.

God: New Beginning of Life—Ending of Life—Fresh Breath for the Earth.

Bells will toll, rings can be heard all over the world of God's message—Love of God—Laughter—New Beginnings with Me in mind. Fresh hearts—Solution of Old. Lazy will go and the Z will vanish—Lay in wait for My message—Act on My message. Be ready to ring the bell. Hear My voice—it will be stronger than ever and know I love you. My love through you will love others, and they shall pass it on.

Hear My Cry. Peace in the World. Be patient. Learn to love yourself more, so everything you do, you do for love. It takes time. Work on it one day at a time. Your willingness is the key.

Dear God:

In this ever increasing high-tech world of computers, laptops, cell phones, blackberries, iPhones, iPods, HDTV, digital cameras, camcorders, CD and DVD players, and GPS navigation, it occurred to me:

If families never talk to one another, who has time to talk to you?

God: Everyone can, but not everyone does. I am open to anyone who will listen or talk. I will address their concerns and worries and wash their cares away, if only they will ask. I cannot do my work if people will not ask. **What I wish is for people to tune out of technology once a day and tune Me in.** I will be grateful and hopefully they will learn to be.

High-Tech World

Excess is ruining lives, and I am here to teach those who care to listen; **excess is only access and does not feed the soul.** The time will come when *things* mean nothing and then what? Just maybe they will come to Me and I will be waiting with open arms. People must learn on their own. It is the only way people can really get to know themselves. What we do not learn in this lifetime, they will learn in the next. **My hope is people will come to Me and get clarification of what they need to access *themselves.*** I only have the best intentions for anyone who comes to Me. They are a gift as I can be to them.

Use technology for the good of man and use Me for the good of yourself. I am more technical than any technology and can show you what you really need. My thoughts and prayers are with everyone whether they know it or not. Come to Me and I will teach you the *technology to your soul.* **Loving yourself allows you to love each other, which is my wish for all lifetime.** We have destroyed much and must get back on track before it's too late. Pamper yourself and you pamper Me. Fill yourself with love and know the powerful benefits. It becomes a ripple effect of love that is far more powerful than technology for the human race. Know I am with you and love you.

Geri: That was awesome. My heart is filled with wonder about you, and my eyes are filled with tears of happiness at your expression and love. I wish more people would listen to *the word.*

God: They will in their own time. The more bells, the more powerful spirituality will become. Thank you for being a bell and continue to help others.

Dear God:

What do you mean by being a bell?

God: Bells ring and bells chime. Chimes are chatter from those who know Me and share My love. **Sharing My message is one of the most important things you can do for Me. It is My only advertisement, and I shall be grateful.**

Dear God:
What would you like me to know at this time?

God: *Eminent is bliss. Bliss is the beginning of blessings. Blessings that are yours to own. Know you are one with the light and can be who you want to be.

Access the wisdom I have stored in you and refresh yourself. You are in the beginning of new life. Life that has more meaning to you, your family, and friends. Be wise and shine within your *confines. Glory will grant those who share their wisdom. **Be gracious and compassionate to those less fortunate in health and spirit than you. Teach that they can have it by coming to Me. Heal your heart, mind, and soul and regain a new beginning.**

Be mindful of trespassers who wish you ill will. Be cautious of evil and keep your eyes on Jesus. Sun in shine of light and bask in the glory of God. Your will shall lead you the way, and I will be grateful for your dedication.

I know it is not easy to change, but change is the only way—a way that compliments your life and gives new meaning to your day. You can choose evil or you can choose Me. **My way honors you and gives you hope, love, and peace.** I wait for you with open arms and will stay with you as long as you ask. Be strong and ask that we join in life together.

Dear God:
How would you suggest we open our heart to you?

God: A simple willingness will show you the way. Open your heart, and I will lead you to a *soul of love.* Ask and you shall receive. I am waiting, if only you will ask. Trust in Me and I will show you the way; anger will disappear, and fear will dissolve. Know I am with you and love you.

Have the courage to seek My knowledge and love, and open your heart. I am here for each one of you who ask. **You open by letting go—letting go of anger, fear, and hatred.** How do they serve you? How content are you in your life? Be willing to change and come to Me. You are able to be who you want to be, if you are willing.

See yourself through My eyes—that you are created in goodness and have faith that together it will happen. Acknowledge the wisdom that is given to you. Pay attention to the message I send you. Be alert to changes that take place and acknowledge *I am on your side.* How you see yourself is what you are. Who you are is how I see you—a being here for a higher purpose that you must be willing to accomplish. Be worthy in who you are.

Take pride in how you walk and talk, and relate to one another. Our hearts were once pure and hardened by sadness and anger. Let Me help you help yourself by being willing to receive Me. I ask that you help yourself through Me and know I am here for you. Changes can take place and will take place if you will open your heart to Me for love.

Dear God:

How does one become one with you?

God: Imagine two *entities merging (ghostlike *entities). That is what has happened with each one of you. I have merged with you far before you were born. My powers are your powers, and you are able to tap into them when and if you choose. Imagine someone giving you a magic wand full of wonder and powers. That is what I have given you by being with you, inside of you, and all around you. **Be silent and listen to your insides and negate what does not serve you well.** Imagine if you could replace it with what you wish for yourself, and you can. Act according to your plan. Know your actions have consequences. Act in the manner before the consequence. Be wise to the ways of the world and better your ways to a better self and a better life.

Imagine all what you wish for in your life, a life of meaning and purpose, not about *things*. **Change your thinking to Mine and know you can get there through Me. Change the way you act and talk and walk and treat other people. Treat people as you wish to be treated.** Get outside yourself and your drudgery, and see the big picture of what you say and do will affect others. Affect others in a positive way and know positive will be returned to you. Start slow and see what happens.

You will slowly start to see the difference your attitude has on others and how their attitude back is different.

Don't expect change overnight. People will see change and you continue to be consistent. Believe in yourself and know you deserve good despite what you have been through in your life.

I am one with you all of your life. Unleash the wand and explore the magic.

Dear God:
What would the universe like me to know at this time?

God: That you are unique in who you are. **That your weave is uniquely yours and in conflict with no one else's.** Your godly purpose is waiting for you with open arms so you may share it with the world. A world that is able to change through people like you who are willing to take the risk. Changes that affect generations of people who are starved for soulful food and wish to do good and be good but do not know how to accomplish their mission.

Show them; tell them they are able to be what they want to be if they are willing to make the changes. Changes from *corruption to *conviction of living the life they wish it to be. Act now and do not wait. **We are all of godly threads and sewing the seeds of love is your answer.** Seek now the truth and the light and the love of your inner being and know you are worthy.

Feel the love I can give you and know it will not vanish. You are my lamb, and I shall take care of you, if only you will ask. I wish to love you and take care of you and for you to pass it on. Open your eyes to the truth and go where you shine. **Step out of the dark and be willing to know your heart's desire.**

You Are Unique

We are all one trying to do our best, but we must recognize the truth and face it. Be joyful and shed unwanted energy. It serves you no purpose and will destroy you. Allow love to take its place and echo your heart's desire. Be free of *bondage and delight in knowing you are who you want to be.

Dear God:
Divine design? What exactly is that?

God: What makes a person unique in their own way—their wants, their wishes, and desires. Their very being. ***Divine design*** is a weaving of oneself, a one and only design, full of wonder and glory. People are born with gifts they live all their life to discover. If they would just come to Me I can reveal them without wasting so much time.

Geri: What is my *Divine design*?

God: Are you kidding? What has grown inside of you for the past twenty years? **A unique gift to figure out what cannot be seen. To know the heart is the decision maker.** Few people travel your route and come out so well.

Geri: Am I really that unique?

God: I think you are. That is why I chose you to write a book; to teach others it can be done. **A new perspective to get people to think, to experiment, to take chances.** Despite what people might think, I love how you arrived at your conclusions—*you came to Me.* Testing as you are you continue to come to Me and not give up. You are persistent.

I like that. They are some of my best students, the hardest to train, but the most dedicated.

Geri: Where do you see me in five years?

God: Wherever you want to be. What I want is only part of it. The other part is up to you. How good do you want to listen? How much do you want to put into action?

Geri: I see your point as usual. I always said you know how to make a point. Thank you.

Dear God:

How do we accept each other as we are and not try to change one another?

God: To try to change someone is *futile. Everyone needs to learn on their own accord. If we only work on our own issues everyone would get along better. Life is a nonending lesson—lessons of evil and good, of appreciating one another. What good does it do for people to tell us what to do when we don't believe it or know for sure for ourselves. **Allowing each other space to grow is one of the greatest gifts you can give.** Accept them with their faults, as we all have faults. Who are we to tell others how to live. **Live the example you wish to portray, that is all you can do.** Be thankful for your knowledge of wisdom and know more is on the way if you desire to become better.

Accepting challenges is part of grace and how you deal with it. Loving them is your best ally. Watching struggle is teaching everyone that no one is perfect, and we are all trying to find our own way. The more people struggle the more they must learn to live in *harmony. ***Harmony is getting out of your own harm's way.*** Know you are only human and set your ego aside to learn new, better ways at which to handle life and relationships. You will learn only if you are willing, and your will, will help you live a better life. **Open your eyes and realize everyone has problems, and see to it you solve your own and not each others**. Time builds character, and eventually you will see it is the only way.

I will help you, if only you will ask. Grace is in space and allowing others to be themselves flaws and all. Know you are loved as you shall love each other. Listen and do not preach. Listen to yourself. Tend to your own needs so you may help others if they ask. **Accept others and you accept yourself.**

Geri: Thank you. Such sweet clarification. Again, back to self-acceptance. How simple if only we could get it.

God: You will. My dedication with love is what I wish for you to pass on.

Dear God:

How do we love our neighbor when it seems sometimes they give us every reason not to?

God: Think of your neighbor as yourself. How do you wish to be treated? **You will solve a lot of problems by loving them and finding out your similarities rather than your differences.** Find out same common ground and grow from there. **You would be surprised to learn one small similarity will dissolve all other problems.**

Know we are all in the same boat, and we must learn to get along. **Dissolve a lot of your own problems, and others will not upset you so much. Your anger attracts anger.** Flush away unwanted anger and look for the good in each other. Small acts of kindness go a long way. Willingness will guide you.

Move if you have to, but know you carry your anger with you. Look inside and ask what you are contributing to the feud. Understand there are life lessons everywhere we go. What is the lesson that needs to be learned? Look deep inside. Are they reflecting the very thing in you, you dislike about yourself? Be shy in blaming others and ask yourself, am I doing everything I can to get along with my neighbors?

Be grateful you are alive to have a neighbor, and treat people as you wish to be treated.

Dear God:

The older I get the less resilient I am to the suffering and sadness of others. How can we cope, be compassionate, and not let it get the best of us?

God: **Compassion is a God-given gift.** Where would society be without compassion. People in the need of love and help seek it through compassion of others by what they have learned from their own suffering and sadness. That is the lesson that is to be learned.

We must recognize the positive side of suffering and realize it is for the good of man uniting in fellowship. Fellowship bonds those who have learned from the sadness and then pass it on in a positive manner. It is all for the good of mankind. If we could only concentrate on the positive verses the negative one would see the good of suffering and sadness. We are a society that wants everything happy and shy from unhappiness. Embrace the lessons to be learned from being unhappy. **Realize self-growth is hidden in such sadness.** Understand you are a better person for having experiences of pain and loss and know you can serve others through your sadness.

Love those who are suffering and in pain as they will remember the gracious gift you have given them in a time of desperate need. They will remember and pass it on, therein lies the beauty of it all.

Life is not meant to be a rose garden. There are thorns along the path. Learn from them and know they have their purpose. Life is a *contradiction of beauty and pain, and what you do with it makes you who you are. Live life in stride and know the rose blooms after a thorn. Enjoy the bloom while you can, and always know the rose will bloom again if you nurture and care for the needs of the roots.

Geri: Thank you. Again you place a positive slant on what we view as negative. The spiritual view always makes one understand a universal plan.

Dear God:

Sometimes you give me so much to sort out. I feel strong one minute and the next day another *plethora of emotions, and I have a hard time handling it.

God: Such is life. The age you are at brings problems to those around you. You are their strength now as the next generation is your strength. It's how it works.

Geri: But I have no children. What will I do?

God: People make their own families—biological is only one kind. There's no promise they will help you either. Don't worry about that now. Get through one day at a time, and talk to yourself and Arlin on a positive level. It will keep you from falling in.

Emotions come in clumps, and the clumps are hard to sort out sometime. Sometimes they are boulders, sometimes gravel, and the other times sand like the sand of time. Turn over the timer, and see you are full again. Use that time to strengthen yourself and others and always know you can get there through Me.

It's a period of struggle for you and Arlin right now. Befriend each other, be kind and generous with your time. Support him all you can, and he will be pleased. You will come out of this stronger and wiser and more compassionate to others. Be patient for you are human, and it is natural. Stay in the moment and do the best you can and know there are brighter days ahead.

Geri: Thanks, it helps to hear you say that. I try to be strong for everyone and sometimes it's just too much and even misread as not compassionate. It's like I can't win sometimes.

God: You are winning. Look at the big picture and what you have. Most people live a lifetime and never achieve a tenth of what you have. Some of this is still the small stuff, and you can't do a thing about it.

Geri: I know, but I still turn inside out emotionally.

God: Would you rather change places with these people?

Geri: No

God: You see it can get a whole lot worse, and you are very lucky in your life.

Geri: You are right. I guess I need to quit crying and get on with life. Tomorrow will be a better day. I just know it will. Thank you for your gracious wisdom and happy belated birthday.

God: Thank you.

Dear God:

Why is everything such a fight? Something that should be simple takes so much time. Businesses misrepresent themselves and businesses have no integrity anymore. What is the problem and how do I handle it?

God: You handle it by being loving and patient. They are just doing what they are told. Greed has changed society and broken down *integrity. **Where an individual would cooperate, their business has other plans to get out of you financially whatever they can even if it appears dishonest.** They are in business to make money. Life isn't easy. Technology has changed the ease of doing business. Where you could once talk to an individual you now get a machine and frustration sets in. Unfortunately, the squeaky wheel gets results. You've already learned that. Now accept it and just be nice about it.

Learn who you want to do business with and who you don't. **Support those who treat you well and leave the rest.** It's all a game to get your business. Don't play the game with the thieves.

Geri: But how will I know who the thieves are?

God: By what they put out to attract you. **Honesty does not have to lure you. Character does not have to lure you.** Be particular who you honor with your business.

Geri: That's easier said than done.

God: Is it? Slow down buying. It will simplify the problem. Learn who treats you well. Leave the rest. Go back to kindness. Drop the frustrating businesses.

Geri: I see, the more I entangle myself in business the more times I get mad?

God: Of course. It's mathematics. **Involve yourself less in business and involve yourself more in Me.** I will show you how to cut down on your frustration. I will show you how to stay calm and accept this is the new normal whether we like it or not, and you have to learn to handle yourself better. Just do it and don't get so emotional about it.

Geri: But I'm a female. We get emotional about everything.

God: It's not necessary. It's a choice. **Slow down when you get upset and remember it's not their fault. It's business policy.** You will get more with a slow, low voice and be persistent. Quit judging how you would do business, herein lies the problem. Greed does not rule your life, and so you cannot accept it does others. Big mistake. Accept that they are different and deal on that level. Once you accept it, it will be easier for you. Now with that in mind, solve the next problem and see if it isn't easier for you.

Geri: Thank you. I learned a lot as usual. I will take your advice.

Dear God:
How do you have time for me?

God: I have time for everybody. I can be many places at once.

Geri: Good for you!

God: So can you, by your note cards, phone calls, teachings. Look how your energy is in other people. That's how I can be with everyone *in what you leave behind.* Make it good, take it slow, watch their face, feed their heart, and leave them a good morsel to chew on. People need that now; in fact, they are starved for it. People have gotten so off track on what is important. Help Me do my work. I get tired, too.

Geri: I guess I'll have to view encounters with others differently.

God: You pass it on, they pass it on, so on, and so on. It's a domino effect. That is why it is good to touch everyone in a spiritual way. You never know the ripple effect you have on someone. We need all the ripples we can get. Some of the most unlikely characters will listen the most, so you never know. It's a gift you give that needs to be shared from person to person. Make an impact and do it with a smile. People will respond positively.

Geri: I've already noticed things opening up to me regarding business; where I expect to get a no, I now get cooperation and yeses. What is that?

God: **That is love expressed through everything you do.** Enjoy, reach higher, it's a great ride.

Geri: Really enjoyed our chat. I got a lot out of today. Thank you. Thank you.

God: You are welcome.

Dear God:
I'm learning so much about spirit from everyone around me.

God: **There are treasure chests full of whatever you are looking for from people all around you.** Ever heard Ask and you shall receive? It's true. People have history they love to share if just asked. They love passing on what they know and spreading the love.

Geri: I'm so blown away by the abundance of spiritual wealth if you just ask.

God: That's all it takes. A slight curiosity can become a guru, a guru who can teach millions. **It costs nothing, and it's a decision only you can make.** Nobody forces you. No one can talk you into it. **But openness to it can change your life.** "I once was blind and now I see," these clichés are much more than that. They are proven and have great merit. They hold generations of power that has been passed down.

Dear God:
How do we learn our life's purpose?

God: Look deep inside; ask yourself what am I here for? **You are born knowing your purpose and then we forget as life goes on.** Our purpose is to serve God in a style that fits your profile. A style that is as natural as breathing so that it never feels like work but rather a reward. Each person can find their purpose, if only they will come to Me and ask. Ask and you shall receive. Receive and you shall extend to others. Others will be grateful for the knowledge and pass it on. That is why it is important to figure out; it feeds everyone's soul, including Mine.

Happiness awaits the brave who wish to learn. Fear of the unknown prevents many from learning. Conquer your heart as you ask questions. Know I am with those who wish to learn. **Be not afraid as fear is a perception and not the truth.** Be *diligent in trying.

Greatness is in each of us, and I will give you the power to succeed. Fear not your doubts, but embrace them knowing I am with you. Enjoy the journey of learning, knowing you are helping others along the way. I encourage the courageous to ask as many times as it takes. Learn to trust what I teach you and inform you about yourself. Encourage others to open their heart and ask what their life purpose is. Learn from them. People working together heightens energy and awareness.

Trust those who speak the truth. **Know your purpose awaits you if you are willing to dig deep enough. Taking time to find it shows me you are serious.** I am pleased when my children discover their gifts. Find your gifts and execute them and many other gifts await you. My greatest joy is to share My wealth, and I wish to extend the desire in you. Ask, receive, extend.

Dear God:
How do we know our fears, and how do we tackle them?

God: **Know them by knowing yourself. Know yourself by coming to Me so that I may teach you the *laws of love*.** Laws that *abide your soul and teach you that you are loving and able to be who you want to be. **Dispel negative energy.** Ask yourself what troubles you and decide it is no longer of service to you. Discount those who add to the negative and engage in the positive people. Anchor yourself and stay on track. Begin to love yourself and be proud of your accomplishments. Take care in what you say and do to people and recognize their response.

People will begin to see the change and be curious. Tell your story and worry not that they believe. Be strong in your *conviction and allow the changes to go forward. Your willingness rewards you, and your outer world will change caused by the change in your inner world. Do not doubt where it comes from. Be cautious that you do not take credit, for I can take away what I grant you if you abuse your privilege. I am here for your glory and Mine and do not dispute where it comes from.

Do not be afraid of your fears but tackle them so they no longer destroy your life. I am one with you and am here for you. **Freedom is facing your fears and opening your heart,** for I shall teach you all you need to know. Learn from what does not work for you and know there is a better way.

Dear God:
What are the laws of love?

God: There are as many angles of love as there are angleworms in the earth.

Start by loving yourself. The changes are a miracle one cannot perceive unless they experience the journey. **The *transformation enlightens one to compassion and generosity towards others. A true miracle takes place within one's soul, and honor is restored to oneself.** The energy is translated to those they come in contact with. It vibrates alone and echoes sentiments of learned wisdom.

People take notice and wish for some of their own. *Inquisitive minds will begin to think of new ways for themselves. They begin to question their life and their ways. They begin to dig deeper within themselves and wonder how they can improve their life for happiness and peace. Small changes will take place, but the difference will add up to *conviction.

Over time thoughts and hearts will change, creating harmony and tranquility if wise minds pay attention. Gather your thoughts and feelings on paper and study them from time to time. **What is not working for you? Know there are better ways. Excel in the areas that are working for you.**

Negotiate with your mind and change negative to positive and come to a peace within.

Angle towards love and get to know the feeling. Anything less will be uncomfortable. Know it shall pass with your eye on peace. **Be willing to change and know if one can, all can, as I have made you all the same.**

Dear God:
How do we obtain peace within?

God: **Peace within is obtained by loving yourself. Loving yourself is obtained by letting go of the negative and holding on to the positive. Peace within is a desire and a willingness to make the journey.** Time will change who you are and peace within will grow inside of you. Harmony will take shape and destruction will disappear. Conflict will cease, and your heart will have a lighter load of anger.

The journey depends on you. How willing are you to compromise? How much do you want peace within? I am able to help you if you let Me. **The road can be short and the road can be long.** That depends on how much you are willing to listen and learn. Your life will change and others will see the difference. You will also be teaching along the way. Others will be curious and want to know your secrets. You will then share *the word* with them.

Sharing your story is powerful and successful to those who know your will. I would be honored to help you and in turn you will show others peace within.

Dear God:
Help me with self-love. I guess I have more to go. What is your definition of self-love?

God: Self-love is in every cell of your body, your entire cellular structure that shines from the inside to the outside. **Love yourself and dissolve your fears.** You have come so far, but there is more to go.

Geri: Define the areas, please, so I know where to focus my energy.

God: **Come to Me. Feel my love, absorb it. Know how it feels.** Share it with others and receive it back. It's an endless exchange of energy between beings.

Geri: In what areas do I still show signs of fear?

God: **In your daily living.**

Geri: How?

God: Where you won't go. What you don't do. What you lack confidence in. You know these areas already. There is no need for me to tell you.

Geri: I see your point. There are areas of lack of confidence. If I embrace them with love, that's all it takes?

God: Yes, of course. Remember that puffball of peace that went off in your body years ago from head to toe? That's what love needs to do—dissipate your body from head to toe. When you do you will shine brighter and stronger, and get more of what you want by accomplishing your goals.

Geri: A perspective I hadn't known before.

God: I know. That is what I am here for, to give you clarity and peace about your fears.

Geri: I noticed that I see children and the younger generation in a different light. They seem precious and endearing to me now. I have really never looked at them in this way.

God: They see you differently, too. Two energies exchanging a higher energy of appreciation. That's good. You are beginning to embrace the universe as it is meant to be, with love.

Dear God:

Julie, just days ago, had a stroke on the way to my home. She says she was able to park the car with safety and call her husband on speed dial, all with your guidance. She asked me to thank you the next time I meditated. So, thank you for being there for my very special friend and some of your very best work.

God: **Your friend is also very special to Me.** Her work for Me has proven *unprecedented, and I appreciate her as well. Few people dedicate their life for My work as she and her husband have done. I am honored by their dedication, as they are a beautiful example of what I can do in the lives of those who wish to ask. **Followers are My friends, and I consider**

them two of My friends. Thank them for being there for Me. They are a fine example of strength, love, and dedication, and passing it on. I am honored to have them on My side and wish them the best. Tell them I love them and will continue to be there for them. They are a fine example the way in which people should live life. I am proud to know them and love them.

I appreciate the appreciation. My spirit is restored by such acts of kindness, and it is My wish people will pass on the same act. **A simple thank you is powerful and not forgotten.**

It rewards those who have the words spoken to them. It's a *validation for all that is done for someone and all was worth it for having heard "Thank you."

So, in return, thank them for thanking Me. I will not forget such sweet sentiments.

Dear God:
How can being appreciative change our lives?

God: What you will discover by being appreciative is love in return. We all need to feel appreciated, and love is the reward. **It is an exchange of appreciation and reward, and what that is, is an exchange of positive energy. Positive energy translates into better relationships and that means we all get along better.** Tell someone you love them and really mean it. Watch them appreciate the gesture, and love is returned. We need to appreciate the little things in life like daffodils in a field and a bug on a tree; the fact we have breath to breathe in order to be able to appreciate. **Being appreciative is a choice of positive energy.** We think we have no control but we do, and we need to be thankful for all we have in our life, good and bad, so that we may learn to be a better self. When our best self comes forward, good is created and passed on. It is a conscious effort. We are here only for a short time on this earth, and a good word to someone can go far and wide.

Jot down daily appreciation. Read them back periodically. See how fortunate you are. Know a positive attitude in life has far more advantage than a negative one. Take baby steps, and you can become a more loving human being by being aware of the appreciation that has been gifted you.

Know you are loved, know I love you, and ask Me for guidance and how to become appreciative. I will show you countless ways to better yourself and your life, if only you will ask. Know I am only here to help you along and comfort your pain. I am ready to help you—are you ready to receive it? I wait with open arms for those who wish to learn by opening their hearts.

Geri: Thank you. Another way for a better life—an attitude of gratitude.

God: Don't be *apprehensive but appreciative, and you shall gain much.

Dear God:

My friend Lola asked me to meditate for her. Should she go on her trip or should she be by her dad's side at this time of surgery?

God: You already know the answer to that. If you answer for Lola, it does not allow her to trust herself. She needs to learn to trust herself.

Geri: But she is hurting so much now. I would like to be able to help her through you.

God: **What would help Lola is to help herself by taking care of herself, eating correctly, exercising, drinking lots of water, and addressing her problems rather than running from them.** She is in this position on her own recognizance. Had she been taking care of herself, she would be able to make this decision with confidence by now. She's running scared, and only she can fix her problem.

Geri: What would it take for her to move on?

God: Acceptance. **Acceptance of the changes.** She already knows this is best, but she constantly second guesses herself. She is a bright woman who is in her own way. Tell her to get out of her way and allow the healing to take place. Accept people's love, accept My love. She is very loved but discounts it as it is not the man in her life. She has love all around her but is not soaking it in and allowing her to heal. She has to figure out the physic hook and cut it. She knows more than anyone how much better off she is, but she continues to hold on. Ask her why. Now weigh it out. Is it worth continuing to be miserable over? This is why she got the divorce—to stop the misery. Now she continues to treat herself the same way—destructive. **Until she loves herself she will not fully understand the magnitude and benefits of her divorce.** Tell her I love her, and I will help her if she comes to Me.

Geri: Thank you. I understand everything you said. I only hope she will.

God: She probably won't, but that is why *TRUST* is the word of the day.

Dear God:
Can you tell me about the physic hook?

God: A physic hook is the hook that prevents you from moving forward. **Once it has its hook in you it will not let go until you allow it.**

What negative thoughts from your past prevent you from moving forward? Look inside and dig deep—deeper than you have ever dug before, and you will find the physic hook. What you do not want to look at most and continue to look away from.

What is buried deep inside you that causes you *dysfunction? What sadness and anger have you hidden away? Until you face them and come to a peace within you will not move forward in harmony.

It is very difficult to unfold but valuable for you, your health, and others. Know you are worthy and can with My help. I shall show you a new perspective and guide you to peace within.

Relationships will prosper in purity, and you shall learn to love yourself. Know you can have a clean heart and dignity can be restored. **Value yourself enough to take the journey and cut the physic hook.**

Dear God:
What are the benefits of forgiveness?

God: What aren't the benefits of forgiveness. Interestingly enough, forgiveness has many more benefits than nearly any word there is. **Forgiveness is necessary for peace within, a choice that is only yours to make. Forgiveness allows us to get along with people, have good intimate relationships, and raise children with a clean heart.**

The mistake people make is staying stuck in the negative. They are unaware of the decay of the soul causing friction in their life. **Discovering the soul's secrets is the focus of forgiveness.** Address what is not good in you. Know you are worthy and can change. Love can conquer all. Be dedicated to a life of harmony and know you can get there through Me, if only you are willing.

Forgiveness is a release of anger and dread and fear, and recognizing it is no longer of value to you. Be brave and open your heart to the changes that can take place. Love yourself enough to make the changes. My hope is your awareness will enlighten you to show you the way, if only you are willing. **Stop being stuck and be alive in Me.** *Bondage will change to freedom, and your heart will be free to love yourself and one another. Forgiveness is the key to *sacredness.

Dear God:
Will you please give me
your definition of the soul?

God: I thought you'd never ask. The soul is the very essence of *who* you are, your very being. Your outer is your shell and the inner is what lives on and on and on.

Your soul is your desires, your needs, your hurts and your pains, your joy, and your peace. Your soul is all of these things. That is why it is important to discover its importance so you understand what drives you. **Looking inside is looking at your soul and Me.** We are one together, and I will show you what your needs are rather than your wants. Your needs will fulfill you, and your wants temporarily sustain you.

Discovering your soul is at the root of all change and the beginning of new life of meaning and purpose and peace.

Shuck your wants and understand your needs by discovering your soul and Me. There are far greater riches that are waiting for you, if only you will ask. Riches with far more meaning than any money can buy. A freedom that you have yet to discover that *bondages now hold you in chains.

Remove the links one by one and know that they will add up to a freedom you have never known. Freedom to love and help others less fortunate. Meaning to the important lessons in life as simple as kindness to others. **Be proud and peaceful in who you are by discovering the very essence of who you are……your soul.**

Dear God:
Why don't I feel like this is a remembering, as you say? It all seems new to me.

God: Unlikely that you feel like this is new to you. You have known it before as I have told you. **It's not like an *aha* but a feeling of complete comfort and *resonates with your soul.** Old spirits know this; new spirits are still learning. Keep taping into your resource soul, and you will begin to feel such familiarity with what you find. Old news is new news to those who do not accept it. That is not your case. All your meditations make perfect sense to you, a common sense for man to follow. This is a *remembering*, a comfortableness that follows the words and thought process.

You are misunderstanding the word *remembering*. What feels right and is in tune with your body, mind, and soul is a remembering. Appreciate your acceptance. Those who do not will not go forward quickly in wisdom. Know you are on the right track by understanding the words to your meditations. The more you ask the more you will learn and understand what a remembering is. You have only scratched the surface of what we are capable of together.

A Remembering

You are wowed by what you have learned so far. You ain't seen noth'en yet. We are an amazing duo who can reach out to other duos and accomplish things you cannot imagine. Expand your thought process and broaden your horizons to more amazing accomplishments. You and I can do anything we set out to do. Be clear on your goals and allow the race to begin. Hold back nothing and watch how we can take off. Only you are stopping this from happening, and only you can change your thought process. You are a powerhouse capable of much more than you think. Trust in yourself and Me and hang on for the ride. Astonishing things are ahead if you allow them to happen. Set your sights clearly and get out of your own way. Magic can take place if you allow it to.

I am here for you—to guide you, to love you, and to comfort you whenever you need Me. Time spent with Me is well worth your effort. I will fill you with confidence and trust for Me and for you. You are a supreme being as all My people are. Believe it as I know it and begin the race to *who you really are*.

Dear God:
How should we address society's *dysfunctional families?

God: We are a society of *dysfunction. Functioning in a disassembled manner in which is damaging to society. To move from *dysfunction to function in an appropriate style would be valuable for families to learn.

Geri: What exactly do you mean by "functioning in an appropriate style"?

God: **Families must work more as a team.** They are disassembled, and the parts would work better if they knew they were part of the same machine. **Teamwork is the key. Each member must know they have value and are important to the family.** They must know they are loved and respected. They must address a problem as a unit and play out their role. Reward is in store for those who do. **Problem solving builds character and character builds trust.** Each family member must know they can trust one another for support. *Dysfunction will dissolve.

Steps must be taken slow and one day at a time. Maturity needs to occur from parent to child. Parents must take a good look at themselves at what they are teaching by their actions. Sometimes it is necessary for children to make the choice their family does not have their best interest in mind. This is a most difficult decision, but one that needs to be made. It is at this time the abandoned family has an opportunity to learn if they wish. Families have chosen their position far before they reach this earth.

Geri: Why do some people choose such difficult roles to play on earth?

God: It's what needs to be done, and they are willing. Willing to teach and willing to sacrifice. They are lessons each must learn for the *evolvement of themselves and others. A view that is hard for humans to understand. The most difficult roles teach us the most and have the greatest rewards. **People choose the role to evolve knowing what good it will do them.**

Geri: That's amazing. We must step back and see a much larger picture in order to understand.

God: Yes, you are beginning to understand. That pleases me you are willing to try. I love that you are seeing *dysfunction is not a negative term, but a positive necessity for the *evolution of man.

Dear God:

In these hard economic times what would you like to say to bring comfort to your children?

God: That we are all in this together. It is time more than ever to unite in fellowship and extend your hand to the less fortunate. Concentrate on the positive gifts in your life, and know we will come out better and stronger in consciousness than before. Know I am with you all and am here for anyone who seeks My love and comfort.

Unite your own family members by spending time with them and telling them they are special to you. Show them that they have God in them and all around them. Your lives will be fuller for having known Me and stronger for having called on Me.

Use this time to ask yourself *what* really matters in my life? Reprioritize things of meaning and place your time and energy in what you decide. Know you are wise for researching your soul to what you really need rather than what you really want. Meet your needs and fill your soul. Ask yourself *who* really matters in my life? Make sure they are at the top of the list, and the time spent with them reflects their priorities.

This is a time for reflection in your life. Use it wisely for the good of your soul. Rest on My shoulder and know I will be here for you. Place Me as a priority in your life. Spend time with Me and get to know Me, as I may know you. Together we will get through the economic times and will be better off for reprioritizing *what really matters in our life.*

Dear God:

Our world is a world of schedules. We view our time as tomorrow, next week, next month, or maybe even next year. At the importance of understanding *evolution how does the universe view time?

God: Here is how it works. **Time is of no *essence and no importance.** *Evolution is based on eternity, so hence there is no schedule, no time; it has no meaning. Give this day your importance and do not think about tomorrow. Tomorrow is just another day, a day that will eventually become today. That is the day we need to concentrate on, as it is the only day we have control over. **Plan only for today for eternity is beyond our comprehension.** Learn lessons based on today, remember them for tomorrow, and change your ways to Mine. Be still and look for answers to better yourself.

Your children and children's children will be affected and so is the *evolution of man. The change of evolving to a better human being of morals, values, kindness, generosity of wisdom, helping one another, being with one heart with Me. Changes are slow and difficult but necessary and important. It would please Me to know people are trying, understanding how they affect their family and others for years to come. Awaken your heart and know I am here to help you. You are important to Me and I want to help. Each life has the ability to grow in Me and change to a better life.

What do you speak to your children today? How do you act around your children today? Know what you say and do will affect them all their life, and be passed on to their children and grandchildren. Be wise in your decision making. Think and act in a godly way. Heal your heart and know life has many blessings waiting. A weak heart can be made strong through Me.

Evolve yourself into today and your teachings of a better you and *evolution shall take care of itself. Are you the best you can be? Are you the person you want to be? Angle your life to your heart and know therein lies the key of love.

Dear God:

What if all *denominations were removed, and we are all one man under God. What would happen?

God: People would not know where to go or what to do. They are programmed by labels and most of them are followers. Take away the titles, and they don't know what to do with themselves.

Answers are all around us, but we don't look; we just follow. If more people would seek their own answers the *denomination would not be necessary. People would be stagnant and not know what to do with themselves. **They need to be shown they are alive in Me.** That is why it is important for people like yourself to teach others to come to Me. They do not need a title or *denomination to hide under; they just need Me.

God's message needs to be relayed in many, many ways so that people begin to get it. It's the repetitiousness from all angles that will convince some. Others will never have the confidence or trust and that's okay. They can go to their community church and feel good they are doing God's work, and they are. I need those people, too.

Spark in others what I have sparked in you. Again the domino effect shall take place. Trust that it will continue. People must do their part and know it will carry on through many people.

Children's children will grow with new thought patterns. Generations can be affected. Know your work through Me is important and will change lives. The more you trust, the more I can teach. Be humble in what you receive and pass it on. Be grateful for the wisdom I impart on you.

My work is special, and I am proud to entrust you with it, as I know you will use it for the good of mankind. Keep a pure heart and maintain the temple in which it lives.

Dear God:

We are taught Sunday is a day of rest. Can you give me your opinion on the significance of Sunday?

God: Yes, I sure can. **Sunday is a day to lie in the sun and reflect on Me. A day of restoration for what the week has put you through.** Time to laugh, to bond, to feel a part of the world, and cry out My name.

For if you do not take time to restore yourself in Me, you have little for yourself and others. My followers need to understand the significance of meeting with Me on a regular basis and restore lost energy and love. I am able to restore and repair if one will ask, and bring you back to new.

Understanding the significance of Sunday is understanding the significance of yourself. Wait not to spend time with Me Sunday, but all days, and restore lost love, repair wounds, settle conflicts, and ease your mind. I am capable of anything you ask, as long as you do your part. People must do their part if change is going to take place. This will not only affect you, but your children and your children's children. Generations may be affected by the positive changes in your life. It may help your future family to live their life easier with a light heart and joy.

Help not only yourself by coming to Me on Sundays to mend your soul, but you can help everyone to see the difference God can make in your life.

Dear God:
I think of Jesus, God, and the Holy Spirit as one. Am I right in my thinking?

God: Yes, you are right in your thinking. **The Father and the Son and the Holy Ghost unite as they stand for peace and love.** Many think Jesus as separate from Myself, but He is of the same energy, molecular structure as Myself. We are all of the same molecular structure and are *one* together. Separateness is what divides us and causes differences among us.

If we had the mindset as one, problems would disappear and strength would take their place. Knowing that your neighbor is you and you are your neighbor. Dividedness would mentally cease and collectiveness would occur as one. United we stand, divided we fall. The truth is deep in this statement.

Change division into divinity and to this *divine self be true*. Get to know yourself through Jesus, God, and the Holy Spirit, and know we are in this together. We are here to get to know yourself and be the best you can be through Me.

Dear God:

I have never given the devil the time of day. Can you confirm there is a devil, and how would you like us to view him?

God: There is a devil—once good, now turned evil. My most prized possession, power drove him to the other side, an unfortunate incident I wholeheartedly regret. I so loved him and his love turned to hate for Me. My heart bleeds for the loss of a once glorious man, a man of power, intelligence, wisdom, now turned to those who loathe mankind. Greed fills his platter.

I long for the day he sees the truth of love, the only way. Hate makes him happy and fills his heart with joy. A more devious human being you will never meet. I am at a loss for words at his betrayal. No one has ever hurt Me as much as the devil has, and I know not what to do. **The world is in chaos over his following of misunderstood minds. The battle is not over with him, and I need many followers to help Me. Love will conquer his quest, and I will be grateful for all who help.**

The Devil

Set your mind to rest. **He cannot hurt you if you do not allow it.** Stray from his wicked ways. **Know you have but one choice that will feed your soul, and that choice is Me.** I will fill you with love which will cast out demons and destruction of your soul. Know you can be healed through Me and harmony will flow into your life, if only you will let Me.

Stay clear of the devil. He will only destroy you and your loved ones, and he will glorify himself. He loves only himself and chooses to be My enemy. **Know you can betray him by loving Me and living a good life. He has no power over your will.** You will only suffer by choosing the devil as your savior. Honor Me and I will honor you.

Geri: Now, I have another question. Was or is the devil a human being?

God: Yes, he can take on many forms. **He is clever and cunning, and can disguise himself easily. Human form is one of his ways.** He is all deceiving and wicked and loves being able to do so.

His manipulative ways are unmatched by anyone and insult everyone. I do not want you to think about the devil and his ways. His energy can creep slowly into you, and I do not want that for you.

Geri: Thank you. I agree and won't ask any more questions concerning him.

Dear God:
Talk to me about the importance of *tithing.

God: *Tithing is misunderstood by those who see it as greed on the part of the church. They do not understand the necessity in which it takes to keep an establishment working which teaches the word of God.

We get what we give. It's the law of physics and the spiritual law as well. Few understand its importance and less establishments are on earth because of the lack of finances. **People must understand it's for the good of themselves as well as mankind that they *tithe.**

The gladness at which they give is also important. A pure heart for the good of man will come back tenfold and bless you in many ways, if only you let Me. Ten/Ten; 10 percent tithing ten times blessed. Count the monetary fragments that come to you after you *tithe. Did you receive them before?

If you loosen your pocketbook, so do I. I know it seems impossible for people to give, but those who have understand the importance. Be careful who you choose to give your money to. Know they are trustworthy and their hearts are in the right place.

Support the kingdom of God and you support yourself. I love you and will take care of you if you honor My word through *tithing.

Dear God:

How would you like us to view death?

God: As a glorious event of coming home. Everyone has to die, and we need to accept it. Life is life and death is death—another chapter of marvelous events. If people would come to Me I could put their fears to rest. We should not feel sad, but rather glad for the person. **Life after death is joy, peace, and love.** Not everyone experiences that on earth in their body. We can all feel glad the pain has ceased, and freedom has set in. We are free from all the bondages our bodies endure. **We should concentrate on the time we have known individuals rather than the loss—what they have *left behind in us*. We should be thankful for the growth they have given us as they cross our paths.** Appreciate, appreciate.

Acceptance is the key. If you do not have acceptance you will not move on, and you will limit your self-growth. You can become bitter or better for having known the person. Be thankful they shared their life with you. Know they are going to a wondrous place far better than where they have been. Cherish your memories, and they will live forever in you.

After all, we do not die; we only change chapters with no ending. You can choose to be positive or negative. Positive will allow you to go on with your life in a happy manner. Negative gets you nowhere, and you cheat yourself of happiness yet to come. Allow grieving and then move on. What we have with an individual never dies, and no one can take it away. Count your blessings, and know I will take care of them and they are safe.

Geri: What about our beloved pets?

God: The same goes for them. They go to a safe place and wait for you as individuals do. They wait for you to come home. **Your gift to them is to continue to enjoy living.** Sadness should only be temporary. Life throws some nasty curves, and we need to be prepared to handle them. If we do not we destroy ourselves and those around us. Come to Me and ask for My guidance. I will help you with your grieving. Difficulty is in everyone's tapestry, and how we continue to weave our life shows what we are made of.

Geri: Thank you. I will talk to you more on this subject.

God: I'll be waiting.

Dear God:
How can we possibly look at what we view as senseless deaths to make them okay?

God: We look at it in a way which is hard for humans to view it. Death is a necessary part of life. Life needs to be sacrificed sometimes. **The way a normal person views death is someone lives a long life and then dies. Other deaths are necessary to teach us about life. Lessons of love and hate and the unknown.**

The pattern of death needs to be broadened and more acceptance needs to take place. Acceptance that there is a plan in the divine scheme of things, and our faith will take us through. **Sacrifice is a very hard thing to accept. I know all too well. It was not easy for Me, but I knew it is what must be done for the good of man.**

Many families have sacrificed much, and they must know I love them and those who have passed on. **Those who have passed on have chosen heroic paths for the good of all mankind.** Be proud of their path and be thankful for having them in your life for the time you did. Be thankful for what they have taught you and given you growth in your own life.

You will understand much more when you reach the other side that you are not able to understand at this time. Your God-given gifts are waiting for you to be discovered. Think about those who have passed before you. How have they contributed to discovering your gift? What have they sacrificed to help teach you? Understand their value through understanding yourself better and thank them for being a part of the plan. **Know you will see them again and all will be understood.**

Be grateful for your time with them and know they await you with open arms. We have been taught one way to look at death. It is time to broaden our view and have faith there is a greater plan for more.

Geri: Thank you. I have never looked at death in this way. You above all know the power of sacrifice. Why aren't we taught more about the benefits of dying?

God: It isn't the human way. It's not viewed as anything positive. **I want you to know death can be positive and play a very valuable role for mankind.** The people who have chosen to sacrifice themselves do not even know, as they may live a normal life. It would be too frightening to be aware of the loss. Early loss is necessary for the *evolvement of man. Life lessons are everywhere, and families have opportunities to prosper from them. It is a choice of appreciation and learning and loving.

Geri: Thank you. Another lesson in acceptance and attitude.

Dear God:

I love how you love me, comfort me, guide me, and advise me. How does this all work?

God: You do not need to know how it all works. Do you know how a car works? It just does. I could try and explain it, but we would not be further ahead. In fact, confusion would surely take place. Just know it simply works.

There are many things that work that cannot be actually seen. For instance, the frequency in the air transmitting from you and all others and all things. You cannot see them, but they are there, and they are powerful and meaningful.

Imagine a racetrack full of cars as they run down the track and the chaos begins. Watch the people react to the chaos in a chaotic manner. **What is emitted is what is received.**

Avoid chaos. Know it will affect you. Revel in harmony and know it will affect you. A comfort level is felt and either centers you or disrupts you. The more one comes in contact with one of these situations and stays there, the more habits will form and take on normal feelings. Be cautious. Ask yourself *how* is this affecting my life? **Pay attention and note** whether your life is heading down a constructive path or destructive path. You have the choice to change that path only if you are aware of what you are doing. **Awareness is the key.**

Be wise in what you do each day and know how it is affecting your life. Change what does not serve you well. You have the power. Watch others around you also change. It is the energy between you that is taking on new form. Be grateful for your awareness and stay on track. **Lives can change no matter what you've been through, but you must take responsibility for your actions and the energy it produces.** Come to Me to guide you to a better way for you and those around you.

Dear God:
Talk to me about the light you always refer to.

God: The light enlightens you to the knowledge I have stored in you. Refresh its meaning and put it into practice. You carry all the tools you need for a better life and a better you. Sharpen the tools I have given you and build a better life; one that has meaning for you and others.

The light will lighten your way to a new path—a path of compassion and love and meaning. Do not stray from the path but continue to put one foot in front of the other for a better you and better ways.

I shall walk the path by your side and guide you along the way. **I am not here to cause problems, but to solve your problems, if only you will let Me.**

I am honored you have chosen Me for the truth and the light. Follow the light of the path and find new ways of which to live, all for the good of mankind.

Conclusion

Find out more about yourself and uncover more truth. That is what soul searching is—pondering life's incidents, misunderstandings, and a desire to grow and become better. Thinking and learning to be a better person.

I want you to have what I have: a personal relationship with God. He is alive in you and waiting to be asked into your life. He cannot do His work if you do not ask.

I HAVE FIGURED OUT WHAT MAN CANNOT SEE WITH HIS EYES. It is a decision of the heart rather than the mind. This is why I wrote the book, so you can have what I have, peace within.

God can guide you to get to know yourself, so you can be better and do better. I want you to have love and joy in your life. Start with a part of your life that does not work for you. Begin slowly and experiment and take chances. God can change your life, if only you will ask.

Are you willing to believe in something you cannot see? Are you ready to connect in a style that fits *your* profile? God can teach in many ways. What are you willing to do?

The choice is yours.

God.........P.S.

Dear God:

P.S. If people buy Answers from God what will it do for them?

God: **What it can do for them is change their life, but it is up to them.** They can be shown I am alive in them and waiting for them to ask Me into their life. **The individual must be willing or I remain dormant in them.** I have the power to unleash what they were born for, if one is willing to try.

I can show them to their soul where old wounds have decayed their life. **Wounds can heal and new fresh growth can occur if one is willing.**

Trusting that it is possible is a choice. Steps can be taken one day at a time showing an individual who they can become, if only they will trust in Me.

I am only here for the good of an individual and wait for you to be the good for Me. Together we are able to build a new life that has far more meaning than an individual can create for themselves alone.

Why not try a new path with Me and see who you can become. To be filled with love and joy is new to many of you, and I can provide that—if you are willing. "Oh come all ye faithful, joyful and triumphant, oh come ye, oh come ye to Bethlehem."

God.........P.S.
Dear God:

P.S. Respond to people who think you sound too human through phrases such as: "pamper yourself and you pamper me," "I get tired, too," "feeds everyone's soul, including mine," and "I am pleased," and using the word we.

God: I have made you. I know how you think and act and respond, and I am only communicating in a way I know you will understand.

Geri: Is there a danger in people thinking you have feelings?

God: Only those that wish to nitpick. Of course I have feelings; I gave you feelings. How do you think I communicate

How Do You Respond to People Who Think You Are Too Human?

with each one of you? Through feelings. **Feelings are my connection to you and the power through you.**

Unfortunately those feelings have negative angles and those are the angles you must avoid. Look for the positive and carry on in life with that in mind. Forget such nitpicking and know it does no good.

God........P.S.

Dear God:

P.S. What are your thoughts on documenting meditations?

God: Well it sure proved valuable to you. Had you not written My words millions of people would not benefit from them. The detail and meaning in each sentence is valuable and would get lost in the thought process over time. Writing information down has a merit all its own. It is a visual that has substance and just is. It is a proof if you will.

Thoughts and feelings are powerful, but if you lose the thought you've lost the feeling. Writing down meditations allows you to revisit My thoughts over time and new meaning lies between sentences as we grow.

I put much thought into what I say to you so that it may mean many things to many people and will have substance with growth. **Keeping My thoughts on paper is valuable for personal growth. New meaning is found from time to time and self-growth is important for Me to know how to guide you to your needs.**

What are your thoughts on documenting meditations?

Begin by asking Me into your life. Document later. See your growth through words on paper and know there is an energy on paper of My love.

Documenting meditations dictates growth. Growth of you and Me together and proof of what we can accomplish, if only you will ask.

God........P.S.
Dear God:
P.S. Am I missing anything you would like us all to know?

God: Just know that I love you. You are all special to Me, and I would hope I am to you. **Feel what is in your heart and know there is more than what man can see with his eyes.**

The power to feel and communicate is as strong as any visual object. It is capable of accomplishing more powerful things. **Know that the power within, between you and Me, contains unlimited possibilities if you are willing to look My way.**

Understand I have only good things in store for you and want the best you can be. Know we are able to accomplish anything you desire together, if you allow Me to guide you. **Are you willing to look my way and connect an energy you cannot see?** My love is pure and strong for all of you. Pure in *intention and *conviction.

I would like you to look at what you need to know, and that is looking at yourself and figuring out what you really desire to be in your life. Your talents are waiting to be discovered and fulfilled.

Coming Soon:

Guidance from God
Restoring your soul

and

Sit in silence and listen
Restoring the hopeless, depressed, and suicidal

More Messages from God through Geri Cruz

Book colors

I consistently received visual colors for the book cover of *Answers from God*. When I looked up their meaning I discovered why:

- Pink..........Love
- Yellow.......Mental process
- Peach.........Higher level of consciousness; eases transition between worlds

Answers from God is a book about a relationship of higher consciousness, based on love and a new thought process.

*Dictionary

Abide...dwell, reside, stay, live, accept, endure, submit
Agnostic...unbeliever, skeptic, doubter
Apprehensive...uneasy or fearful about something that might happen
Bondage... the state of being bound by or subject to external power or control
Concise...succinct, short, brief, pithy, pointed, summary, compact
Confines...imprison, incarcerate, jail, detain, cage, restrict, bound, limit
Conservation...maintenance, protection, keeping,
Contradiction...deny, refute, explore, overthrow, dispute
Conviction...belief, persuasion, faith, opinion, view
Corruption...demoralize, degrade, bribe, contaminate, spoil
Counterproductive...tending to defeat one's purpose
Denomination...name, title, class, kind, sect, persuasion
Diligent...application, industry, activity
Dysfunction...impairment of function, malfunctioning
Eminent...height, altitude, elevation, distinction, rank, importance
Entities...thing, being, whole, unity, existence

*Dictionary

Essence...being, substance, entity, reality, nature, life
Evolution...evolvement, unfolding, growth, expansion, development
Futile...ineffectual, vain, idle, useless
Harmony...agreement, order, symmetry, tunefulness, unison, peace, friendship
Inquisitive...questioning, curious, prying, meddlesome, busybodyish
Insidious...operating or proceeding inconspicuously but with grave effect
Integrity...honor, uprightness, wholeness, completeness, oneness
Intention...intent, purpose, decision, plan
Intrigue...plot, conspiracy, scheming, espionage
Meditate...to engage in thought or contemplation, reflect
Oblivious...unmindful, unaware
Perpetuated...commit, inflict, perform, do, practice
Physic...a medicine that purges
Plethora...overabundance, excess
Preservation...embalming, curing, pickling, salting, smoking, canning, dehydration
Provisions...something provided or supplied
Recognizance...a law or obligation entered into
Resonate...to resound (echo)
Sacredness...hallowed, sanctified, holy, dedicated
Tithing...the tenth part of goods, income paid as a tax for the support of church
Transformation...change, alteration, conversion, transfiguration, metamorphosis
Unprecedented...new, novel, unheard-of, original
Validation...substantiate, confirm, approval

3-2-13

Prayer For Me

in all places dark
shed light

in all places that are weak
shed strength

in all places that are scared
shed courage

in all the places of pointing ①
aside

shed gratitude
where I fear to tread
walk w/ me

in all the places I hesitate
shed support

Remind me I am a
Divine Design
Part of a Divine Plan
and you need me
to shine

where.
in all the places
where ignorance is
shed wisdom.

wherever there are lies
within
shed truth.
wherever I am blind
~~increase~~ my vision
~~shed light~~

So @ the moment
of death (~~physical~~ emotional)
will you regret
anything or relationship
you choose not to
heal?

So @ the moment

can you heal any
wound preventing
your freedom of peace at the present moment?

Made in the USA
Charleston, SC
26 February 2010